HEITOR VILLA-LOBOS

BACHIANAS BRASILEIRAS NO. 5

Solo Saxophone (or C instrument) and Saxophone Quartet

Arranged by Frank J. Bongiorno

I0803435

AMP-8066

First Printing: February, 1993

Associated Music Publishers, Inc.

DISTRIBUTED BY
HAL•LEONARD®
CORPORATION
7777 W. BLUEMOUND RD. P.O. BOX 13819 MILWAUKEE, WI 53213

BACHIANAS BRASILEIRAS NO. 5

Aria (Cantilena)

Heitor Villa-Lobos
(1938)

duration: ca. 7 minutes

Arranged by Frank J. Bongiorno
(1991)

* The parts include three versions of the solo part: B♭ for soprano saxophone, E♭ for alto saxophone, and C for any treble instrument.

5
7
9
dim.
dim.
dim.
dim.
dim.

12
allarg.
14
1 A tempo
f
mf
16

19
allarg.
2 A tempo
p
cresc.
pp
cresc.
pp
cresc.
pp
cresc.
22
allarg.
A tempo
p
pp
pp
pp
24

HEITOR VILLA-LOBOS

BACHIANAS BRASILEIRAS NO. 5

Solo Saxophone (or C instrument) and Saxophone Quartet

Arranged by Frank J. Bongiorno

Solo Soprano Saxophone in B♭

AMP-8066
First Printing: February, 1993

Associated Music Publishers, Inc.

DISTRIBUTED BY
HAL•LEONARD® CORPORATION
7777 W. BLUEMOUND RD. P.O. BOX 13819 MILWAUKEE, WI 53213

BACHIANAS BRASILEIRAS NO. 5

Aria (Cantilena)

Heitor Villa-Lobos
(1938)
Arranged by Frank J. Bongiorno
(1991)

Solo Soprano Saxophone in B♭

HEITOR VILLA-LOBOS

BACHIANAS BRASILEIRAS NO. 5

Solo Saxophone (or C instrument) and Saxophone Quartet

Arranged by Frank J. Bongiorno

Solo Instrument in C

AMP-8066
First Printing: February, 1993

Associated Music Publishers, Inc.

DISTRIBUTED BY
HAL•LEONARD®
CORPORATION
7777 W. BLUEMOUND RD. P.O. BOX 13819 MILWAUKEE, WI 53213

BACHIANAS BRASILEIRAS NO. 5

Aria (Cantilena)

Heitor Villa-Lobos
(1938)

Arranged by Frank J. Bongiorno
(1991)

Solo (in C)

HEITOR VILLA-LOBOS

BACHIANAS BRASILEIRAS NO. 5

Solo Saxophone (or C instrument) and Saxophone Quartet

Arranged by Frank J. Bongiorno

Alto Saxophone I in E♭

AMP-8066
First Printing: February, 1993

Associated Music Publishers, Inc.

DISTRIBUTED BY
HAL•LEONARD® CORPORATION
7777 W. BLUEMOUND RD. P.O. BOX 13819 MILWAUKEE, WI 53213

BACHIANAS BRASILEIRAS NO. 5

Aria (Cantilena)

Heitor Villa-Lobos
(1938)

Arranged by Frank J. Bongiorno
(1991)

Alto Saxophone I in E♭

HEITOR VILLA-LOBOS

BACHIANAS BRASILEIRAS NO. 5

Solo Saxophone (or C instrument) and Saxophone Quartet

Arranged by Frank J. Bongiorno

Alto Saxophone II in E♭

AMP-8066
First Printing: February, 1993

Associated Music Publishers, Inc.

DISTRIBUTED BY
HAL•LEONARD® CORPORATION
7777 W. BLUEMOUND RD. P.O. BOX 13819 MILWAUKEE, WI 53213

BACHIANAS BRASILEIRAS NO. 5

Aria (Cantilena)

Heitor Villa-Lobos
(1938)

Arranged by Frank J. Bongiorno
(1991)

Alto Saxophone II in E♭

HEITOR VILLA-LOBOS

BACHIANAS BRASILEIRAS NO. 5

Solo Saxophone (or C instrument) and Saxophone Quartet

Arranged by Frank J. Bongiorno

Tenor Saxophone in B♭

AMP-8066
First Printing: February, 1993

Associated Music Publishers, Inc.

DISTRIBUTED BY
HAL•LEONARD® CORPORATION
7777 W. BLUEMOUND RD. P.O. BOX 13819 MILWAUKEE, WI 53213

BACHIANAS BRASILEIRAS NO. 5

Aria (Cantilena)

Heitor Villa-Lobos
(1938)
Arranged by Frank J. Bongiorno
(1991)

Tenor Saxophone in B♭

HEITOR VILLA-LOBOS

BACHIANAS BRASILEIRAS NO. 5

Solo Saxophone (or C instrument) and Saxophone Quartet

Arranged by Frank J. Bongiorno

Baritone Saxophone in E♭

AMP-8066
First Printing: February, 1993

Associated Music Publishers, Inc.

DISTRIBUTED BY
HAL•LEONARD® CORPORATION
7777 W. BLUEMOUND RD. P.O. BOX 13819 MILWAUKEE, WI 53213

BACHIANAS BRASILEIRAS NO. 5

Aria (Cantilena)

Heitor Villa-Lobos
(1938)

Arranged by Frank J. Bongiorno
(1991)

Baritone Saxophone in E♭

HEITOR VILLA-LOBOS

BACHIANAS BRASILEIRAS NO. 5

Solo Saxophone (or C instrument) and Saxophone Quartet

Arranged by Frank J. Bongiorno

Solo Alto Saxophone in E♭

AMP-8066
First Printing: February, 1993

Associated Music Publishers, Inc.

DISTRIBUTED BY
HAL•LEONARD® CORPORATION
7777 W. BLUEMOUND RD. P.O. BOX 13819 MILWAUKEE, WI 53213

BACHIANAS BRASILEIRAS NO. 5
Aria (Cantilena)

Heitor Villa-Lobos
(1938)
Arranged by Frank J. Bongiorno
(1991)

Solo Alto Saxophone in E♭

31
rall.
34
rall.
3
Più mosso
mf
ten.
simile
37
ten.
ten.
ten.
40
ten.
poco string.
rall.
4
Grandioso
A tempo
43
rall.
A tempo
rall.
A tempo
rall.
46
A tempo
rall.
A tempo
f
49
liberamente
Tempo I
mp
53
56
60
allarg.
A tempo
allarg.
pp

rall.
rall.
3
Più mosso
poco string. rall.
4
Grandioso
A tempo
rall.
A tempo
rall.
A tempo
rall.
A tempo
rall.
A tempo
Tempo I
allarg.
A tempo
allarg.

35
3
ten.
simile
37
ten.
ten.
39
ten.
ten.
41
poco string.
rall.
4 Grandioso
A tempo
43
rall.
A tempo
rall.
45
A tempo
rall.
A tempo
rall.
A tempo
f
48
f
pp
Tempo I
p
52
55
59
allarg.
A tempo
allarg.
ppp

28
31
rall.
3
Più mosso
34
rall.
simile
mf
37
4 Grandioso
poco string. rall.
A tempo
rall.
A tempo
rall.
A tempo
rall.
41
46
A tempo
rall.
A tempo
f
f
pp
50
Tempo I
2
55
58
61
allarg.
A tempo
allarg.
ppp

25
28
5
rall.
rall.
3
Più mosso
mf
36
simile
39
poco string.
rall.
4
Grandioso
A tempo
43
rall.
A tempo
rall.
A tempo
rall.
A tempo
rall.
47
A tempo
f
f
pp
51
Tempo I
pp
54
56
60
allarg.
A tempo
allarg.
ppp

rall.
3
Più mosso
rall.
mf
ten.
simile
ten.
ten.
ten.
ten.
poco string.
rall.
4 Grandioso
A tempo
rall.
A tempo
rall.
A tempo
rall.
A tempo
rall.
A tempo
f
liberamente
Tempo I
mp
allarg.
A tempo
allarg.
pp

31
rall.
34
rall.
3
Più mosso
ten.
simile
mf
37
ten.
40
poco string.
rall.
4
Grandioso
A tempo
43
rall.
A tempo
46
f
49
liberamente
Tempo I
mp
53
56
60
allarg.
pp

26
28
31
rall.

34
rall.
3
Più mosso
mf
f
36
ten.
simile
39
poco string.
rall.

4 Grandioso
A tempo
rall.
A tempo
rall.
42
45
A tempo
rall.
A tempo
rall.
A tempo
48
liberamente
f
mp
pp

51
Tempo I
pp
p
pp
53
55

57
59
3
61
allarg.
A tempo
allarg.
pp
ppp